Successful Married Life

10 Little lessons every women must know
- "Married Life is easy if you KNOW how to handle it"

Our schools don't teach it

A.M Kaywills

*"Married life is easy and simple,
To make it more sweeter know how to handle it before
you face it. " Sana Kayavil*

*"After long time I got a right book for my wife to read"
Wilfred Antony*

*"Married life is a new change in your life,
It's easy and lovely if you know to sweeten it."
Aneesa Ashir*

*"This book enlighten me to handle my husband after
15 years of married life."
Sara Kamal*

*"This book will help all women who love to take her life
to heights"
Indu Prasad*

Contents

Preface

Married life is new episode of life which needs much knowledge to bring it to sucess, but sadly no schools teaches it. I believe this book will help you to handle married life more intelligently and positively. It has never been easy to suggest a woman how to run her family life, but I felt the need to share the knowledge that I have gathered over the years about family life which may help young girls to make their married life successful, as I saw many divorces happen in my family circle and society due to silly reasons which are purely lack of knowledge to handle the married life situations.

This book can be read on two different levels. First, it may be read by married women who can check out the lessons which they can find what is missing and secondly one who is planning to get married. I had made this book very minimal pages so that every women can use this as a quick handbook.

This book is designed to make your life peaceful, lovely and rich.

Chapter 1: Eye to Eye

Dinner with your partner paints a common picture enjoying a great menu at the restaurant table, and posting its pictures in social media. Sorry, a dinner like that is not what we are talking about.

The dinner we're talking about is all about a dinner date to make a magic moment of eye to eye, heart-to-heart and a sweet dish served with love.

The sole purpose of the dine-in is to have an eye-to-eye moment, It's all about creating a special magical moment of love exchange of eyes to eyes. It is said that eyes speak deeper than words, something beyond talking and dinner is simply a reason to sit facing your partner to make this magic happen.

For having a very personal and romantic time, there is no place better than home, where you can have ample time together than in any restaurant. That being said, the question is — When was the last time you had a romantic dinner with your partner? If you cannot remember, probably now is the ideal opportunity to whip one up; there is no need to wait for any special occasion for it to happen. Whether you're looking to treat yourself or do something thoughtful for your partner, let these tips below are your guide to your at-home dinner bliss.

Clear Your Schedule:

Set the stage for your romantic dinner by making sure the time is only for the two of you. If you have children, arrange for a babysitter to watch them away from home, or ask parents or friends for help.

Decide On The Location:

You can always set the table in your garden if there is one. This can be very romantic, provided the season of the year is right, and that you have a nice, bug-free garden. You can also plan for dinner in the kitchen, but clearing the kitchen up to set the mood can be a bit troublesome to make it presentable for the event. The whole point is to pick a location where you don't normally have your meals, so the night feels special. If you have a "fancy" dining table that you never use, now's the time.

Plan To Use Your Fine Dishes:

Pick a set of nice crystal glasses and fancy plates that adorned your cabinet till now, napkins, and silverware that you never use because they're out only for special occasions. Well, the occasion is now -- bring them out and take pleasure in how much they add to the romantic atmosphere.

Choose Your Romantic Decorations:

Flowers from your garden, rose petals, and unscented candles will do the trick — options are plenty and you just have to be creative to make the most of it. Remember that candles energise and ups the vibe, so you can light a few candles and place them on or
near the table. Flowers, such as elegant roses, are almost as important. They look good at the table and elevates the whole ambience, whether it is something extravagant or simple.

Dress Up:

Before starting your dinner date, take time to have a nice shower, and put on some perfume or cologne. Dress up just like you were going out to dinner. Put on some casual, but beautiful clothes, so that you look refreshed and effortlessly attractive. Your partner will appreciate the effort, and the night will feel even more special. Just make sure you decide on a dress code with your partner before the date, so you both look equally fancy.

Avoid All Distractions :

Make a plan to avoid all distractions so that you and your date can be free to enjoy your delicious meal and each other's company. Apart from having the kids managed by a babysitter or parents, free yourself from devices by switching off phones, television, and radio,and focus only on each other. If any big game or a favorite live show is scheduled for that night and one or both of you is interested in it, you may want to reschedule your date so that you aren't distracted. Once all the distractions are put away, you can focus on enjoying a personal romantic evening.

Taking an effort to create moments makes life sweetest. And moments like that can be wisely used to share love and care. Such moments are missing in today's world. It can't be blamed on anyone. To start with, topics about relationships and values are missing from the school curriculum. We are missing that training to have insight on how to lead a sweet and blissful life as a couple. The lack of such knowledge to be blamed for having unstable relationships.

Right now, let's learn to make this magical day happen. A day to make your relationship deeper with magic bounding eye to eye dinner. Plan a day which is convenient for both of you within a week better for your eye to eye dinner date. If you are newly married and have no clue about cooking, chill — you can still make it with a food delivery order, do it with a Swiggy order so it is easy to handle that part.

The focal point here is to have dinner as per your liking and don't miss to include your partners likes too. Then it all goes down to having it served romantically. Keeping a candle will change the tone of your dinner setting. Remember that all this effort is to make your partner feel the love you have towards him. Now that the mood is set, sit opposite each other and enjoy your date with him and have light talks about a subject which keeps the mood in check, especially about a moment you both liked, or ask about the last best day he remembers and keep the mood up. Or even you can start with our magic moment we planned for this day.

Let's Do The Magic:

Stop talking, let your eyes do the talking. If you don't get his face towards you, you can spice things up by making a game up by asking him to look into your eyes. Once you have his attention, play it around — "I am going to tell you something with my eyes, let us see if you can find it out.". Keep looking into his eyes and chant in your mind repeatedly, I love u man! Let it be like that for 3 to 5 minutes without breaking your eye contact. This will let your partner see deep into you.

The magic of Dine with the eye is a powerful moment maker. Secret behind the magic is letting his eyes read your love through your eyes. Our mind is directly connected to eyes and it can speak deep and lot without opening your mouth. Human beings yearn for love and love it when expressed freely. A man wanders his eye for love, all we need is to guide it inside ourselves. Without such moments in life, his eyes and heart always will be in an endless search for an expression of love from anywhere. With this eye dine you train him to follow your eyes and express his subconscious mind with your love, as it is said, eyes are roadways to one's inner self.

Ask him if he can make out what you wanted to tell him through your eyes. If he doesn't end up giving the right answer, you can still let him know that was 'I love you man' and make him feel your love towards him, the matter is not about the ability to find the answer but to train him to look into your eyes and feel your soul.

With this eye magic, take the conversation the way it flows. Make it a point to look into his eyes and talk. And avoid any debate topics or complaints, in which case simply smile and divert the topic by suggesting to keep that discussion for later. And you can also tell him that, "For now, I just want to look into you". The whole mood of the evening, the ambience and the conversing eyes will end up binding you both together as if in a magic spell and your partner will learn to look into your eyes and feel you.

Chapter 2: Touch Magic

Winning one heart is quite a natural process, it happens naturally. But due to current life situations and work pressures, we all are filled with lots of activities which keeps everyone under stress, especially everyone around the world is facing stress due to work or business issues.

If we study the current family problems, 90% of the cases we find are due to pure misunderstandings or failure to win each other. Hence, regardless of you being a new or old couple, the knowledge to express love will be pleasurable and bounding.

This chapter is all about letting you know how to express love other than by words, a language used by the entire living life force in this universe to express their love for each other. An expression of love known to all, but used sparingly in the current world of a busy life is - the touch of love.

So let us talk about the importance of a touch of love that intensifies your love. The universal truth is that, without love, everything is boring and seems worthless. So winning the heart of our loved one is the most joyful act to do. You can win his mind in many possible ways, among which the most powerful way a woman can express her love is with touch.

Touch of Love

Touch is the most intimate expression of love and touching a man's head is the most powerful of it a woman can use for a man to turn into his submissive version. With a simple touch, you will realize that in the hands of love and affection, such a strong man is as submissive as just a pet. Running hands through his hair makes him feel loved, or more deeply cared. Such care every man wishes for and this action makes a man behave as her pet. Every woman should keep doing this to her man as the result is sweet, but be mindful of the topic that you choose to talk. Choose light, romantic and warm topics or else it better be a meaningful silence during this. Pat on the head soothes a person as such an act of affection like hands
on hair is encoded to be soothing since everyone's birth.

If you want to make a guy fall for you, you have to know how to touch him the right way, while making sure your advances are welcomed. There are different reasons for touching a guy, depending on the stage of your relationship with him. If you're only getting to know him, you may just want to touch him to show affection. If you want to spice things up, you can touch him to be flirtatious. And if you're already dating or living together, then you'll need to know how to touch a guy to pamper him.

Holding his hand while walking or sitting

This act lets him feel that you are always together. A great time to Just be together without an agenda. You don't have to talk about anything. Sometimes it's just nice to be present for each other, with nothing but the sounds of nature and light footsteps. Silence and solitude can be good for you sometimes.

Your walk as a couple may not be the most earth-shattering thing you do as a couple, but it will make a lasting impact.

Hug Is Most Powerful Touch Technique

Yes, a hug is indeed THE most powerful technique among all the touches that we discussed till now. Body language sometimes can tell you a lot about one's emotions towards your partner. Also sometimes it is much easier to express your feelings to the people you hold dear. Hugs can be sort of a greeting at times, but when you hold your partner tightly in your arms and don't let go easily, that's something entirely different. You can do it in many different ways to express a range of emotions.

Hugging might be easy for some but a fairly difficult thing to do for a few because of various reasons. You might be shy, or you aren't sure that you will convey the right message to the person you want to hug.

But here you can find some ways on how to embrace your partner emotionally in the right way.

Neck Locker Hug

This sounds like a regular hug, but you should hold him closer and put your arms around his neck as his face ends up in your chest. This is very romantic because he can feel your heart closely. A woman takes up a man in a very warm embrace to her chest to express the deepest and passionate love that she holds for him. When this happens, hold for a while and once you release, look him in the eye and smile affectionately, don't look away. With this truly special hug holding a man's face to your chest, makes him feel the depth of love you hold towards him, far better than any words could.

Such emotional moments are cornerstones of any relationship and lack of which is one of the most common reasons of hate between couples.

Hug Him From Behind

This hug is unique, it shows more care. It can be done while he is sitting or standing alone. You can hug him from behind which is romantic, and it can be used in various kinds of situations; for example, you can make it playful, by jumping and suddenly hugging him tightly, or you can just hug him slowly from behind while he's doing something else. It is wonderful to display someone affection when they least expect it. Unexpected things are the best. If you are much shorter than your partner, it will be even cuter. Always be mindful of what your partner is doing before moving on with it. Don't jump him by hugging him like this while he's on something important and needs to concentrate, because you might startle him. So just be careful and choose the right moment to cuddle your partner romantically from behind. A wakeup hug is the best way to start your day filling it with love, which makes him feel reassured that someone is always behind him with lots of love and care. Such acts need only a few minutes but it works deeper than a year of unnecessary talks.

Every man has got a child hidden inside them, who loves the caring expression of touch. If we are to watch cats, dogs and love birds we can always find them doing their touch of love. It is natures way of expressing love to each other. Everyday sex may not be possible, but a warm and gentle hug of a few minutes will mean volumes. Enjoy giving your hug and see the change in your love life.

Chapter 3: Positive Attitude

Successful life with your partner can only happen by maintaining a positive attitude in the relationship. That happens when both parties are committed towards creating a positive and caring atmosphere. We can find most successful marriages where the families nurture positivity.

The ratio of positive to negative thoughts is a major factor in overall happiness. Your brain is constantly monitoring the emotional tone of your thoughts, if too many negative thoughts cloud your brain then the brain responds by creating stress and thereby sadness engulf you. When you add more positive thoughts, your brain will respond accordingly and as a result you will be more relaxed and happy.

This key knowledge is for anyone who wants to know how to make sure their marriage succeeds. To have a successful marriage that lasts forever, there is plenty you can do to strengthen your marriage and wisely bring positivism to life which improves the chances of success.

To make that happen, at first you should learn how to cultivate a positive attitude. Every situation has the potential to be converted into a positive one. All it takes is just a simple smile. Keeping yourself silent during many negative occasions is the easiest positive attitude one can take to avoid any problems.

Let's take a look at how a positive attitude will help your marriage succeed.

Attitude Really Is Everything

There is a saying that attitude is everything - and honestly, sometimes it can sound like a bit far fetched. If you harbor feelings of resentment, anger, or animosity towards your partner, it is much harder for your marriage to succeed. Think of it this way: If you had a friend who constantly nagged you or put you down, you wouldn't want to be around that person very much. On the other hand, you'd love being around the friend who was always delighted to see you and was fully supportive of you, right?

The same is true for your partner. If you cultivate a positive attitude towards your spouse, you will share a closer relationship, which will be more honest, and nurturing for both of you. Your marriage will become a place you want to retreat to, a space of warmth and support for both of you.

With this reason all my lessons are tailored to create positive moments in life.

Look For The Good In Your Spouse from time to time! Instead of focusing on what frustrates you about your partner, try shifting your focus on what you love about them. Make a conscious decision to notice all the things you love about your partner. If they have an amazing sense of humor or always support you in your dreams, notice that. Enjoy the fantastic moment you had while helping with the kids' homework.

Let your partner know what you love about them, too. A surprise text or cute note tucked into their lunch will make them smile, and remind them that they're loved and valued.

Gratitude

Gratitude sometimes gets cast aside when life gets busy or stressful. It's hard to remember to be grateful for your partner. When faced with challenging situations, train yourself to look for things to be thankful for about your partner. If they take a moment to make you a cup of coffee, or the work that they are doing for supporting the family. Even if there happens to be a time when the situations get the best of it making your partner end up losing his job, make an effort to thank him for his contributions till date and inspire him every way with positive affirmations.

Being grateful to your partner can have a powerful

positive effect on them. Even better, tell them about it! Make sure they know how much you appreciate them. Celebrate the little (and big) things. Celebrating together is a wonderful way to get you both focused on what's good in your marriage. Don't wait to celebrate the big things like a promotion, baby or new home. Although those events absolutely call for celebration. Maybe one of you got some great feedback at work. Take time to notice all the smaller good things that happen in the normal course of a week or month.

Avoid Looking Into Problems

We're so used to searching for problems in life and skipping over the good stuff. Make it a point to look for all the good things, no matter how small, that are happening all the time.

Then crack out your favorite WORDS or make your favorite meal and celebrate them with your partner. You can even get into the shared habit of listing three good things about each other every day before you sleep at night. It seems simple, but practicing positivity and gratitude is a powerful way to help your marriage succeed.

If you are concerned that you have a bit of negative personality or have the tendency to lean towards negativity, ask yourself the following questions:
Are you a perfectionist? If someone says, "Good

morning," do you wonder what's good about it?
Are you critical of everyone in your life? Do you look at incidents and events from a negative perspective?

Are you quick to say "no" and rarely say "yes" to requests from your partner or kids?
Do you find yourself in a bad mood on a regular basis? Do you dwell on bad things or painful memories?
You can change your pattern of negative thinking. Self improving will help you resolve all your problems.

How To Change Your Negative Thinking Patterns

Even if you are chronically negative, you can change your pattern of negative thinking. However, the one to make a change towards having a better way of handling your chain of thoughts is only you, no other person can make it happen for you.

Here are some things you can do to be more positive:

▫ Avoid negative self-talk and try staying positive. Our negative self-talk affects us in a very powerful way. If we believe something to be possible, we're more likely to make an

effort to achieve it. Whereas If we think
of it as impossible, we won't even bother
trying.

□   Be more open-minded.
When you have a positive attitude about
new experiences, you can open yourself up
to new discoveries every day. It's a great way
to keep your life fun and exciting!

□   Cultivate gratitude.
Gratitude is such a powerful emotion, that
can make your life better in more ways
than one. It's quite difficult to feel depressed
or sorry for yourself when you have the
feeling of gratitude. Tell your partner you
love them and how much you appreciate
them.

□   Do something that makes you smile.
Meet a friend who makes you comfortable
and exudes positivity and better yet -
makes you laugh.

□   Eat healthy foods.
Many studies published have found that a
healthy diet helps a person in keeping a
positive attitude with the help of right nutrition in their diet.

□   Exercise.
When you exercise, your body releases endorphins which in turn leads to have a

feeling of positivity.

◻ Get enough sleep.
Getting a sound sleep for seven to eight hours a night can help you restore clarity and improve memory. "Poor sleep has an adverse impact on thinking".

◻ Help others.
When one person performs a good deed, it causes a chain reaction of other altruistic acts. There is a Chinese saying that goes: "If you want happiness for an hour, take a nap. If you want happiness for a day, go fishing. If you want happiness for a year, inherit a fortune. If you want happiness for a lifetime, help somebody."

◻ Seek professional help.
Seek out professional support if you are unable to manage your thoughts or find that they are interfering with your ability to meet your daily responsibilities or enjoy life.
Counselling and therapy can help you manage yourself, reduce emotional suffering and experience self-growth.

◻ Surround yourself with positive people.
Choose the company of happy, positive

and motivated people and you won't be
able to help but soak up some of that positivity.

□ Use words of affirmation.
Affirmations are positive statements that can help you to challenge and overcome
self-sabotaging and negative thoughts.

How to Help Your Negative Partner

If your partner has a negative personality, you are not responsible for making them feel better.
However, here are some things you can do to help your partner be more positive:

□ Do not take the negativity personally.
□ If your partner rejects your offers for help, don't overreact.
□ Make them spend time with positive people.
□ Invite your spouse to take a walk or do some fun activity with you at least once a week.
□ Acknowledge your partner's accomplishments.
□ Encourage your partner to try new things.
□ Establish healthy boundaries.
□ If necessary seek professional help.

Chapter 4: Forgiveness

Forgiveness is very important in any relationship. Be it between friends, families or a couple. We can re-learn a thing or two from observing children around us. If we look into the friendships children share, we can find something in common. Even though they fight like cats and dogs, they do reconcile after a few minutes. They forgive or forget about it and keep playing. The ability to forgive/forget or to let go is needed for any successful married life.

"If you cannot forgive, then the unresolved hurt will remain like cancer, eating away the very foundation of your marriage."

Often people equate forgiveness with weakness, and it is widely believed that if you forgive someone, you're condoning or excusing their behaviour. However, in marriage, forgiveness is a strength because it shows you are capable of goodwill towards your partner. The very first thing that prevents couples from building trust and emotional attunement is the inability to bounce back from a conflict in a healthy way. The best solution to this problem is to get good at fixing the relationship.

Practice forgiveness by actively thinking like a forgiving person. Avoid holding grudges and declare that you are free to stop playing the role of a victim. After all, we are all imperfect and deserve compassion. Practising forgiveness will allow you to turn the corner from feeling like a victim to becoming an empowered person.

When Forgiveness Is Not Enough

Being able to forgive and to let go of any negativity in the past is very critical in marriage. Additionally, being
able to forgive is a way to keep yourself healthy both emotionally and physically. Forgiving and letting go may be one of the most important ways to keep you and your marriage going strong. Some transgressions are so harmful that a marriage can't survive, but forgiveness can still play a role. Don't Hold onto old wounds, disappointments, petty annoyances, betrayals, insensitivity, or anger. The only outcome from holding onto it is wasting both your time and energy and affecting your life adversely. Nursing your hurt (whether real or perceived) for too long can eventually make it turn into something more—hate and extreme
bitterness. Lack of forgiveness can also wear you down. Being unforgiving takes both a physical and mental toll.

How To - Forgiving Techniques

There are different techniques you can use to find a place of forgiveness when you have experienced a hard time with a partner.

- Dwelling on those thoughts - When images of the betrayal or hurt flash in your mind, refrain from throwing the mistake back on your spouse's face at a later date; don't use it as ammunition in an argument.
- Accept that you may never know the reason for the transgression, behaviour, or mistake.
- Refrain from seeking revenge or retribution - Trying to get even will only aggravate the pain and chances are that this won't make you feel better anyway.
- Remember that forgiveness does not mean that you condone the hurtful behaviour of your partner.
- Be patient with yourself - Being able to forgive your spouse takes time. Don't try to hasten the process.
- Seek professional counselling - To help you let go and forgive. If you are still unable to do so, or find yourself dwelling on the betrayal or hurt.

Power Of Forgiving

Forgiveness does repair the past, while you look upon it with compassion. Holding onto anger and resentment clouds your judgement and end up pulling you in every wrong way possible. Forgiveness gives power to the one who forgives while anger and blame discolours your perception of life. To forgive, avoid thoughts of being wronged. Rather, trust the power of forgiveness to heal the hurt and pain buried deep inside of you. By holding on to pain, you suffer and stay being miserable. To recover and gain a powerful mind, forgiveness is the best medicine which activates your power to heal.

There is a widely believed miconception that to forgive is to mean to forget, which clearly is not the same. Forgiveness is when we find a better way to understand the cause and fix whatever is eating away our peacefull life or make a decision to avoid such unhappy events from happening again. The most important thing of forgiveness is letting go of hatred, and allowing the power to heal for love to flourish again.

How To Ask For Forgiveness

Sometimes we make mistakes, and If you are the reason your partner is hurt, you can ask for forgiveness to rebuild trust in the relationship. Remember to give yourself and your partner time when working through the process.

Show true contrition and remorse for the pain that you've caused.

Be willing to commit to not hurt your partner again by repeating the same hurtful behaviour.

Accept the consequences of the action that caused your partner to be hurt.

Be open to making amends.

Make a heartfelt and verbal apology; this includes a plan of action to make things right.

Be patient with your partner. Being able to forgive you often takes time. Don't dismiss your spouse's feelings of betrayal by asking them to "get over it."

Even you can take some initiative to solve the issue - Find a private, quiet area where you can talk. You should ask your partner to meet you in an area that is quiet and not very crowded so you can talk in private. Choose an area where you both had a good moment, feels like the neutral ground, as you do not want your partner to feel uncomfortable. It can also be a coffee shop or local hang out you and your partner enjoy going to. Meeting in a spot that is part of your relationship makes the conversation feel less awkward. Express regret for your actions, be confident. Start the conversation by expressing regret for what you did. Express your feelings with honesty and let your partner know that you realise what you did is wrong, and it shouldn't have been done. Do not get defensive or makeup excuses for your actions. Instead, let your partner know that you regret what you did and realize it was wrong.

Once you have offered your sincere apology, you should ask your partner if they would be willing to forgive you. Being honest with your words and emotions is the key towards taking the step to make amends. Gaining back trust needs more effort and patience from your side. Express yourself sincerely so that your partner is able to have a glance at the feeling of remorse that you have, of your actions and the readiness to make amends in every way possible. Even if your partner accepts your apology and forgives you, give time for your relationship to recover.

You should take steps to make amends for your behaviour so your partner can move forward positively and start placing their trust on you again. Making amends, even in a small way, can help your partner feel confident and get over your mistake. You may also surprise them with a thoughtful gift or dinner to show how bad you feel about your actions. Choose a gift or dinner that will make your partner feel special and show them how much you care about them.

Chapter 5: Handling Anger

It is very important to learn the basics of how to handle a moment of anger before entering a family life. Many families fall apart upon encountering such an incident or crumbles up in a moment of anger. So learning how to deal with it is very important to lead a family life, as we are humans and situations that might lead to losing one's temper can happen when two people with different personalities embark upon a journey together.

As you may have painfully discovered, anger can be detrimental to relationships. An angry partner's negative attitude and behaviors can drain your energy, leave you feeling frustrated and unheard, and undermine not only your well-being but the overall health of the partnership. But, if you can deal skillfully with an angry partner, your relationship may transform drastically. Here are some effective strategies for dealing with an angry partner.

When you try to control an angry partner, they may become defensive and more uncooperative. It is unwise to respond to anger with anger itself; better to let the other person vent out their pent up emotions and remind yourself that they will eventually calm down. The calmer you stay, the quicker their anger subsides.

Acting assertively is the process of taking a position in which you can express your needs directly and respectfully while considering your partner's feelings and needs as well. When you act and speak in an assertively respectful manner, you are being confident, honest, and open. At the same time, by being assertive, you empower your partner to take their share of responsibility for their actions. People often act in an angry manner because they think they are not being heard, understood, not being taken seriously, or not being appreciated. They might be feeling disappointed and ignored.

To avoid inflaming your partner's anger, it is wise to actively listen to them until you are sure they feel heard and understood. Go beneath the surface and try to understand their deepest worries, and validate their feelings and experiences. Validation is a way to communicate acceptance of ourselves and others. It doesn't have to mean that you are agreeing with everything. Rather, it is recognizing and considering your partner's perspective. The key to validation is being present and genuinely trying to understand your partner. It is not just listening to them, but giving yourself an internal experience of staying true to the situation rather than pushing it away or avoiding it.

Beneath every person's anger typically lies deeper and more vulnerable emotions such as fear, sadness, or pain, which may be less accessible for your partner to address. For a short period, anger serves as a protective shield and makes your partner feel powerful and in control. Yet, in the long run, it holds the power to hurt them from within. This is the reason why it is important to have compassion towards your partner and keep yourself away from blames and accusations. Patience can serve as the most powerful antidote to anger building up within yourself and towards your partner. It entails being wise at the very moment anger arises. It is about waiting and not speaking or doing anything that may be automatic or reactive. Patience and compassion are the foundations of positive energy and co-operation among people.

The phrase "pick your battles" doesn't just apply while referring to military combat; it is also relevant to relationships with partners who tend to get angry. While in combat, military leaders might even be willing to lose some fights so that they can "win the war." They generally don't waste resources and energy on the ones they can't win. In the same manner relationships can be a battlefield of sorts, just because of the fact that individuals have different beliefs, opinions, preferences, and expectations, where exercising restraint is at times is a wise strategy. If you want to, you can find an abundance of matters about which to argue with your partner.

But, it would be your call to be selective and letting go of the least important matters. Remember, it's neither sensible nor practical to fight over every difference you have. You may win the argument, but chances of it being at the cost of your relationship are rather high.

Being responsible for each others behaviors can help your relationship in the long run. When you choose to be responsible in a relationship, it means that you are ready to accept your role in being frustrated with an angry partner and effectively reflect on what actions might trigger their anger. It also means understanding what triggers you to behave the way you do. The more aware you become, the less reactive and more constructive you may become. The result will be a greater well-being for you, your partner, and your relationship. If you realize you played a role in escalating an argument, be responsible and acknowledge your part in making the situation volatile. You stepping up and owning your behavior or reaction may help reduce the tension in the atmosphere and encourage your partner to do the same as well.

When your partner's emotional state is highly charged, their cognitive state may be impaired. There is little point in addressing the issue as long as the dominating emotional state is anger which ignores any reasoning or possible logic. Take time for the negative energy to settle to go ahead with a more rational discussion. When both of you are calm and collected, address the issue that led to your partner's outrage. At this time, they may be more open to listening and understanding. Also, don't forget to apply this rule to yourself. When you find yourself being overridden by emotions like anger or displeasure, take time to calm yourself.

Anger fuels anger, and calming promotes a calmer atmosphere. Don't focus on trying to change your partner. You might end up being disappointed. You can, however, influence your partner and show them the benefits of being calm. You can influence your partner by creating a positive environment that is conducive to cooperation rather than control. You may have heard the expression, "You can catch more flies with honey than vinegar." When if you treat your partner with sweetness, you will bring them closer to you—and closer to understanding how you feel and why you feel that way. This might increase your chances of productive outcomes.

If you apply the above strategies, you may be astonished to see how much the energy between you and your partner transforms and your relationship flourishes.

Chapter 6: Art of Attraction

How To Be Always Attractive To Your Man.

Every woman loves being called attractive, and every man in the world loves admiring attractive women. It is the law of nature and the way men and women are made. Knowing your man's likes, and being attractive to him occasionally keeps love life colourful.

Nowadays illicit relationships have become common, and if you dwell on the topic and research on it, you will find many reasons. Making yourself attractive and appealing to your man is very important in maintaining a vibrant love life. After a few years of marriage, many women stop caring about the way they are presenting themselves to their partner. It's important to find time to keep each other attractive. Being attractive doesn't just imply beauty, but staying fresh and dressed in a pleasant manner also adds to the beauty. So presenting oneself in a well-dressed manner, the way your partner loves, is the most beautiful idea to be attractive in front of your partner.

It is important to remember that beauty is all about perception. What one person finds attractive might be off-putting for another. So we can say that one thing's for sure: there is no single thing that every guy likes when it comes to beauty. However, there are a few things that are guaranteed to set the heart on fire of most guys. First of all, know that it's very normal to notice a change in your man's sexual drive after marriage. The reasons could be many, so don't feed yourself the thought that he doesn't find you attractive anymore. Take the necessary steps instead, to make sure your husband gets in the mood, especially when you want his attention. Don't force anything but trying to make him see you attractive is an important game for your relationship. Be mindful to not get too laid back and lounge around all day in pyjamas or a nightie which gives out an unkempt look. That doesn't mean you have to perform household duties looking like a glam doll. Before you get caught up with the chores of the day or sprucing up the house, take some time to freshen up and make yourself feel good. If you're a stay-at-home mom, don't greet your husband, when he comes home, with your youngest kid's spit-up decorating your blouse. Take the time to shower and look fresh for him when he comes home to you.

But there are more things you should keep in your checklist that make you more attractive.

★ Keeping your teeth white and mouth fresh.
Clean white teeth are a sign of good health and it makes us more attractive to others. So grab those whitening ideas or approach a dentist soon if you have issues with teeth and mouth in general. There is nothing more offputting than bad breath, so once you are at it, make sure to get deep into the issue and seek help. It gives you more confidence once this part is checked out and corrected.

★ Water Magic - Keep your skin's glow.
Glowing skin makes you look more pleasant. For that, you need to drink plenty of water. The best beauty advice one can get in looking beautiful without makeup is to drink plenty of water. We know enough about the importance of Water. Every system and function in our body relies on water. Keep a bottle of water with you wherever you go and keep yourself hydrated through the day.

Drinking a minimum of 8 or more glasses of water helps flush out toxins from your body, and hence your skin looks soft, fresh and clear. It also helps keep wrinkles away. Water is indeed a magic potion that you can rely on when it comes to beauty or health in general for that matter. You can find the best way to consume water that suits you, from the internet. I personally know one hot lady who always carries a bottle of water filled with cucumbers, lemons and mint leaves as detox water to drink. This is a good tip and gives you the nutrients as well as the hydration to help your body utilize and hold onto the water more efficiently.

You can look for more tips to keep you glowing, but there is no denying that the most effective one is water.

★ Sleep Well To Keep you fresh and beautiful.
A night of good sleep is a significant factor in how you look and feel. It's crucial because your body repairs itself while you sleep. Just like you need to charge your cell phone, your body needs to recharge itself. Lack of sleep makes you start your day off with lower energy. To go through the day with your battery at 25%, only leads to added strain and inefficiency. 6-8 hours of quality sleep is vital for you to wake up feeling and looking great. By doing this, you will have a glowing face, less of those dreaded dark circles under your eyes and you'll slow down your ageing process.

The skin produces new collagen when you sleep. Which keeps you away from wrinkles and helps you look younger. A home natural look not only allows your authenticity to shine through, but it's also the best thing you can carry around. It shows how well you look after yourself. Yes! You need to be mindful of essential aspects of your diet, your habits, your lifestyle and your skincare routine.

★ Stay Natural, Be Natural and beauty conscious.
We are what we consume that affects our overall health, what we apply on the surface does the same. Your skin absorbs 60% of the stuff you put on. So make sure to do some research on the ingredients that are present in your skincare, haircare, and beauty products. Keep away from products that contain parabens, petrochemicals, and sulfates that may cause irritation to your skin or make your hair dry and frizzy. It's best to stick to products that contain natural ingredients. Such chemicals keep affecting your health and mood too. Use natural care and oils to keep you moisturized rather than handing it over to chemicals.

★ Stay Fit and Look Hot

Physical activity is so essential for both your physical well being and mental health thereafter. Invest some time in things like hitting the gym, running, doing yoga or going swimming. Scientifically, it is proven that exercise benefits your skin and improves your mood. A minimum of three hours of physical activity per week will result in improving your health. It improves your blood circulation, helps get rid of toxins, increases the amount of oxygen delivered to your skin, provides a boost of endorphins that reduce stress and calm your entire body, including your skin and mood. Moreover, it keeps you looking attractive.

★ Take care of your lips

Studies have found that our lips are considered to be one of our most attractive and arousing facial features. It is also found that drawing attention to them with red lipstick means they will be stared at for an average of seven seconds longer. So if you're looking to feel your sexiest, start taking care of your lips and put on an attractive lipstick that complements you well. The main thing is to keep it well and not end up making the lips chapped and dry.

★ Do avoid Stress

Stress can lead to problems like headaches and hypertension. It can also lead to acne, hair fall and early greying of hair. These are only a few severe outcomes of stress. So while you can't entirely avoid bills, work, your life and all the stress that comes with it, you should find a way to manage it. Meditate, go out for a walk with friends, drink a nice hot cup of tea, listen to your favourite music or make some time for anything you love.

★ Dress Up

Every woman dresses up for other parties and tries to be their best for any guests or while going out. But at home, they just let go and the worst version of themselves when it comes to dressing. Try to bring the mood up by keeping yourself attractive at least while you are done with the day and move to bed, or evening while your husband is back from work. Let him see you as a fresh cute flower.

What you wear affects how you present yourself. Ensure all the clothes you choose fits you perfectly. Stock your wardrobe up with clothes that compliment you and look flattering on your figure. Wearing clothes that are too tight or baggy can be uncomfortable and can add bulkiness to your shape. Clothes that don't fit you well are only ruining your style. Add in some extra effort to find stuff while you shop, that makes your body look flattering and also allows you to breathe.

Being comfortable doesn't mean that one can only look shaggy and run down. Put in some effort to find what is suitable for you.

★ Keeping your mood happy

Your mood is the key to the happiness of you and the people around you. Besides all the external factors, it's most important to keep yourself genuinely happy. The stress and monotony of our daily lives will dim our sparks and make us really distressed and sad. Make sure you take some time out for yourself and engage in activities that bring you happiness—be it painting, cycling, listening to music or cooking. If your mood is happy naturally you are attractive because a smiling face that resonates happiness is the most attractive thing to anyone.

Enjoy the tips and have a great day of your life. Look into your partner's eyes always and smile. It is the easiest and simplest way to make you most attractive.

Keep Smiling.

Chapter 7: Art of Success

The art you must know to keep your husband Rich and successful.

Behind every successful man, there is a woman, similarly, for every successful woman, there is a man behind. It's true in my life's experience. I believe and agree to it that my Eve is the secret behind whatever success I have. It's her understanding and support that helps me bring out even this book. Without peace of mind, no man can do great things. And without his woman's love and care, a man can't attain peace of mind.

How women can help a man to succeed is a vital knowledge a woman should possess. If you know that secret, your family will succeed on every side. With a successful career and family life, you will be benefiting from each other.

So let's look into a few of Eve's key secrets.
"Without the love and support of my wife and children, I wouldn't have the drive to keep fighting to succeed."

Numerous studies have confirmed that our family,

whether biological or hand-picked, can have a major impact on our success. A supportive spouse can be a key part of having a strong career. While some couples work best together when they are both invested in their own careers. Women love to support their men to succeed, and I believe every woman wants their man to be successful.

Knowledge is key: Try and get to know about things that relate to your man, his work/business and his interests, so that you have something other than household matters to talk about. Your man will be proud and you will add value to him in becoming more successful. Also, it helps you to understand exactly how he is tied and what he is looking for next. You can guide and support him too. Which is a great blessing for him to have trusted support back home who understands his work pressure.

Every woman wants her man to be successful. Who doesn't? Seriously, she wants the men in her lives to bring home success, to provide for financial safety to the home. Every Eve wishes her partner to be financially sound. But most women don't know what they can do to make their man succeed.

If you are a working woman, it might be hard to fit everything in. Building a career, keeping up with friends and staying fit usually means that there is hardly enough time left to cook a hearty meal. Regardless of that, making time to ask your partner how their day was, Ironing their clothes and making the bed or doing things for them that would make their lives easier would make a lot of difference. It's not easy to fit into a multitude of roles and that's why we call a woman the powerhouse of every home. The effort she puts in is the power that helps a man to succeed, that's why the Indian culture teaches men that "Shakthi" is his wife.

Only she can still iron her husband's shirts, care for her kids and cook for the family even though she herself would be rather having the busiest days at work. All for the sake of joyful faces smiling back at her. If a married man succeeds, a lion's share of all his efforts will without any doubt be of his wife, because no man succeeds without peace at home.

She powers everything from home. A wise Eve knows that such efforts will be paid back and she will win financial freedom to keep a helper to support her. We find most financially successful families having one thing in common, they complain less and appreciate each other more. Supporting families are the core of a successful man.

Being a man and being successful often comes with a lot of stress. Men put pressure on themselves to provide money for the family, social standing and success. When something goes wrong with a business, in the office, or unseen issues in business can be stressful. With stress, people tend to exhibit odd behaviours that are unreasonable, say things they don't mean and tends not to think clearly. As a smart wife, you can let it go and give him care until he settles off. Always stressful situations can be handled effectively with caring words and not complaints or fights. If you understand your spouse's stress and how it affects his mood, it will help you better understand your man. You will be able to provide them with the support they need to minimize the stress that they are under.

Let's look into some tips which might help you to support your guy to succeed.

DRESS FOR SUCCESS:

Regardless of the industry that your man is working in, it must be made sure that he is dressed to his best according to what his workplace demands. If he is a representative, be it marketing, sales executive or a businessman, he must be required to be dressed in formals and is well presented or in the industrial or construction sector where the dress code is uniform, ensure that he looks his best and fresh every day. Especially if your man is a public servant who has to wear a uniform each day, no matter what industry your man is in, make him feel proud and respected from home to his job. Depending upon the situations that you are in, you can decide whether to take the task up personally or have laundry assistance to help you out. The way a man looks speaks volumes about the way he is treated at home.

Send him to work happily

Starting a day off on a good note is very important as it influences the mood for the entire day. At times, it may so happen that there are certain things on your mind that you want to let out, but the best thing you could do to yourself and your partner is to hold back and refrain from having an agitated conversation before you part for work. Always make sure to leave home on a happy note, and a smiling face. If you are to part for the day after a heated discussion, it will end up leaving both of you frustrated and unfocused on whatever that you are into, be it in both your workplaces or daily chores at home. The argument and its aftertaste will end up leaving both of you anxious and think about nothing but the argument until he/you both reach back home.

The extent to which a simple argument could affect a day might differ for each person. On the work front, being unfocused could lead him to trouble like losing a very big deal. The unpleasant mood in which he is reflects in all his daily activities which in turn might lead him into mistakes that he might not be able to rectify at work and might cost him his job or any valuable opportunity that he might have had. Hence, hold any thought and stop yourself from putting it into words that might lead to an argument till he is back home for fewer arguments and more productive talks to fix what in your mind at night at the fine confines of your home, and settle it before going to bed and have a great moment. Settling issues positively before you call off the day is very important to have a productive day after, else you are keeping another frustrating day for both of you.

All success requires peace of mind. Seeing your man happy and joining in on his happiness, is the best feeling in the world. Remembering that you chose your man for a reason and that their happiness makes you happy will make your role of supporting them a lot more fulfilling.

Another important thing everyone misses while having a busy career is keeping the body and diet healthy. It's as important as peace of mind is. A happy mind needs a healthy body too. So it's very important to plan your family's health as well. Join him in leading proper diets and workouts. Else while leading a successful life with a steady career, financial stability and a happy family, several health issues might click in. Even though we cannot stop whatever health issues there might be, a good and early start to leading a healthy life can help us in the long run. So it's very important to plan your husband's diet and health along with yours, which women are adept at. If you have no such knowledge try to get advice from dieticians over the internet and let your husband join a health club as well, not leaving you to laze around. A healthy and peaceful wife is the master power of a home.

Anywhere in the world, if a married man succeeds, that means he is blessed with a happy family. Simply put, a woman can only make her man succeed, which in return makes her successful and financially secured.

Chapter 8: Fitness and Family

Healthy food habits, fitness and family health is the most important wealth of a family.

Carelessness in the food habits of a family can disrupt the peace of home with many health issues blocking the path. Ensuring that the family's food habits are on the right path is a major task a smart Eve need to manage. The key to having a healthy family lies in the hands of the lady of the house. The success of a family is not measured by wealth amassed by them, but the real wealth of a family is having them in good health. Having every member of the family follow a healthy lifestyle and eating habit can be done by the significant efforts put in by the lady of the family. Indulging in unhealthy foods on a regular basis is equal to sending out an invitation to health issues.

Keep A Healthy Food Menu For The Family

A combination of healthy diet options is required to ensure that you are not losing out on much-required nutrients to your body. So always keep a diet with a combination of dishes. Especially in the case of kids. Parents control their food supply. You plan which foods to buy and when to serve them. Though kids will pester their parents for tastier and colourful options, which might be less nutritious, adults should be in charge when deciding which foods are regularly stocked in the house. Kids' choices are always what's available at home while they are hungry. They'll eat what's available at home. If you stock junk snacks, kids will naturally eat them and build a habit of it. So always try to bring healthy snacks home. Food Time Schedule is important too, improper food timings results in the build-up of a lot of gastric issues.

Schedule Regular Meal And Snack Times.

Putting a menu plan will help to manage your kitchen supplies. This may seem like a little too much planning. But if you keep a schedule and menu plan, it will be helpful in organizing the quality and quantity of food supplies required. It will help to plan supplies to buy and use to cook or serve. Building a healthy eating habit early on in life will be beneficial for the kids, especially when kids are drawn more towards tastier, unhealthier options widely available in the market. Getting kids to enter the healthy eating bandwagon might be easier said than done. But the likes and dislikes begin forming even when kids are babies. You may need to serve a new food a few different times for a child to accept it. Don't force a child to eat, but offer a few bites to get them into trying something new.

With older kids, get them to have a try of one bite. Kids love hot dogs, pizzas, burgers, and macaroni and cheese, ever wondered why? To an extent, they are influenced by what the media is presenting to them as tastier options of food. Kids brains are most attracted to such advertising. But they love trying out new menus. When eating out, let your kids try new foods and they will surprise you with their willingness to experiment with healthy foods. You can start by letting them try all sort of foods. Strictly avoid Soda and other sweetened drinks which add extra calories and get in the way of good nutrition. Water and milk are the best drinks for kids. Occasionally indulging in sweets are fine to an extent, but a clear distinction of what desserts are and how it is supposed to be eaten need to be made clear to the kids. When dessert is the prize for eating dinner, kids naturally place more value on the sweets than veggies, which most kids hate.

As an adult, if you have a sweet tooth and indulge in sweets regularly, your kids naturally follow you. Be a role model and eat healthy yourself. When trying to teach good eating habits, try to set the best example possible. Choose nutritious snacks, eat at the table, and don't skip meals.

Fitness

A healthy soul needs a healthy body. Nowadays with the fast-paced lifestyle and with better facilities, physical activities have come to an all-time low, which can be said as around ten per cent of the average requirement. Great food and a lazy lifestyle is as lethal a combination as it is jumping from a flight without opening a parachute. Please don't wait till a health issue arise, if you neglect your health for a longer period, health issues will for sure be unwelcomed guests who will be there to stay.

Exercise

Everyone still is of the notion that you have to join a gym for you to exercise. The truth is that to have the best exercise in the world, you just need a mat and a yoga instructor on youtube. Yoga is known for its ability to ease stress and promote relaxation. Studies have shown that it can decrease the secretion of the stress hormone 'Cortisol'. Some people practise yoga as a way to cope with feelings of anxiety. There are studies showing that yoga can help reduce anxiety. In addition to improving your mental health, many ayurvedic doctors in India suggest that practising yoga may reduce inflammation as well.

Inflammation is a normal immune response, but

chronic inflammation can contribute to the development of pro-inflammatory diseases, such as heart diseases, diabetes and cancer. Another advantage of yoga is that it could help decrease symptoms of depression. This may be because yoga is able to decrease levels of cortisol, a stress hormone, that can influence levels of 'Serotonin', the neurotransmitter, often associated with depression. Getting a mat for yoga is advised if you have issues with falling asleep. Poor quality of sleep has been associated with obesity, high blood pressure and depression, among other disorders.

Another no gym workout option at home is Zumba. Zumba is a workout featuring movements inspired by various styles of Latin American dance, performed to music. It's become a popular and trendy workout across the globe. Even if not necessarily Zumba, you can choose your favourite dance and enjoy it daily for an hour. The reason Zumba got famous is that it covers workout for

most of the body parts. With a combination of Salsa and Aerobics, there's no right or wrong way to do Zumba. As long as you move to the beat of the music, you're participating in the exercise. And since Zumba involves movement of the entire body from your arms to your shoulders and to your feet, you'll get a full-body workout that doesn't feel like a boring workout session. Another advantage of Zumba is that, since the intensity of Zumba is scalable, you are moving at your own pace to the beat of the music.

It's a workout that everyone can do at their own intensity level. Be it Zumba or Yoga, the world's top workouts just need Youtube access and most of all a bit of dedication to get yourself up and doing it every single day without fail. This workout can be done with all family or alone. The most relevant thing is keeping you healthy is the best thing you can do for your family. With great health, you can stay healthy to enjoy your life. Stay healthy, that's beauty.

Chapter 9: Family and parents-in-laws

If you ask any married person, you will find out one truth about a successful married life that is well connected to parents-in-law. Supportive parents-in-law are found to be one big factor when it comes to having a successful married life. Yes, it is extremely important to develop a good rapport with mothers-in-law. If you succeed in that, you will for sure maintain a very joyful married life. If we are to study the most common issue that crops up between a couple after marriage is related to in-laws, which clearly happens due to failure in building trust and rapport with one's parents-in-law, especially mother-in-law.

The mother-in-law dilemma - the most common trouble a girl faces after her marriage.

The very first step in understanding your mother-in-law is realising that she is the one who has invested her entire life in her family and has been the focal point of the family. Especially when it comes to her son, one needs to realise that she held a major part in her son's life, including his decisions, diet, wardrobe etc all through his growing years. Till the day you enter her son's life, she used to be the one who served him food once he was home, picked clothes for him and even be a part of the decisions he made all through his life. Once you enter the household she might become a bit insecure of all the changes that happen at home and you being the focal point in her son's life and the feeling that she might be losing control over her family.

She, the one who adorned the lead role all these years might feel like being pushed aside and almost replaced by someone younger who is more energetic, younger and the one who is showered with all attention from his son. This transition needs time. Perhaps your father-in-law is as much a villain and gives you more attention and asks for opinions. If by any chance there comes a situation where you and your mother-in-law happens to have different views and both your husband and father-in-law stand by you, she would feel even more annoyed and intimidated. With all the focus on you, the newly-wed daughter-in-law, she might feel like being challenged for her position at her own home. The very first thing you can do is tell her that you, being the younger one, look up to her and be guided by her. This will give her the secure feeling that you are asking for support and help from her and that she still is the one in charge of her home, which makes her feel less challenged by you.

Another thing is - Pieces of Advice from mother-in-law could feel outdated, which might make you feel irritated. But you can't deny the extensive experience that she holds in parenting, running a home and lots of other aspects in life as well. So it is more likely that she might come to your aid in the form of advice of providing assistance when she sees you doing something different to what she does, as she might find it a bit difficult to turn a blind eye to it. The way you do or perceive things might be different than hers, but there is no harm in hearing her out as a person with more life experience and take its better part. Two advantages from this: first is that she will feel happy that her advice was taken which makes her accept you more. The second is that even if her advice is not acceptable, you get to practice your listening skill and not get defensive.

It's difficult to understand what it feels like to be a mother until we become one. And we will become one for sure. Your mother in law is your husband's mother, the crucial part is that she is getting old and insecure and there is no denying that you will also reach there at a later point in life. Just imagine how much your mother-in-law loves your children and your husband and realize that she has a longing to be a part of your life. So include her in your life plans, because tomorrow you will take the same position.

In every household, problems and misunderstanding are bound to happen. It's important to know how you can fix such situations before you prepare to move into it. If you come to know of any issues your mother-in-law has over you, discuss the problem privately to determine the root cause of the issue. Start by explaining that you aren't angry or upset, but simply want to understand if unknowingly your action made her upset and explain to her that it was not your intention to make her upset. There may be an underlying issue that is bothering her, and discussing the problem in a collaborative way will get you closer to solving the problem and feel closer to her, she is a woman like you whose aim is only to secure her family.

In certain cases where the mother-in-law and you had a fight or misunderstanding, get your spouse involved in the matter without delaying which will have a better impact on the situation. Ask your spouse to talk to her if she isn't communicating effectively. If she can't even discuss the problem without starting a fight, enlist your spouse to talk to her. Ask him to calm her down and open up a channel of communication with her. She may simply feel uncomfortable talking to you about her grievances. If she won't communicate constructively, don't engage in an argument. She may likely try to pick a fight and this will create a vicious cycle where you're unknowingly giving her another chance to fight.

Mothers-in-law always stands with her son. Always express gratefulness for your spouse in front of your mother-in-law. If your mother-in-law is often critical of you specifically, try showing lots of affection and appreciation for your spouse whenever she's around. She may relax if she feels like the two of you are both working towards the common goal of making her child happy. That's the main concern of any mother-in-law that her son is in the right hands and being taken care of well.

It's important not to avoid or ignore your issues with your mother-in-law. Later it could turn into serious fights. Talk to your spouse to see if this has always been a problem. If your mother-in-law has always been demanding, or argumentative, you may need to simply work out a strategy to minimize the behaviour and cope with it. If this is new behaviour and it is directed only at you, there is likely an underlying problem that must be addressed. Talk to your spouse to get a better understanding of your mother-in-law.

Don't get ahead of yourself and start talking or arguing with your mother-in-law without consulting your spouse first. If you cross a line or engage in an argument without agreeing on a coping strategy, you may end up offending your spouse. Decide on whether you want to confront, deflect, or avoid the problem together. Always think that with love and care all problems can be solved, issues with mothers-in-law are just simple cases that can be solved with love and care.

Wish you a great life ahead.

Chapter 10: Make time to love you

Everyone is unique and they have their own abilities. It's important to have your time to be yourself. This makes your inner self feel special. If you love dancing, painting, reading, writing or travelling, always try to make time for it. Not giving the time for yourself, you feel empty and miss what you love to do. While you enter family life, your schedule might be tightly packed, but if you are wise enough, you can find time to do what you love to do. The time you spend for yourself will refill your energy and will be able to keep much-needed enthusiasm for you to carry yourself forward in life.

Deep down we all know that it's important to make time to look after ourselves, not least so we can carry on looking after everyone else who needs us. Most women often don't take the time with the excuse of being too busy, or that they've always got the kids with them, or a demanding job taking up the time. There are
always excuses to prevent you from putting yourself

first. If you're struggling to find the time, or know that you need some help in finding ways to prioritise yourself; you are at the right place. It's important to save time and make time for yourself. Let's look into some ideas to save time and how to make that "Me" time for yourself.

Shopping

One of the most challenging things women face in daily life is getting daily supplies. And they spend a lot of time over it too. But if you pre-plan it or give partial responsibility to your partner or use the home delivery for grocery supplies from your regular shopping area, it will save huge time and money. If you have limited free time that is spent having to drag yourself through shops buying birthday presents, food and household goods it might be ideal for you to switch to online shopping. You can now virtually buy anything on the internet - books, toys, cosmetics, clothes, groceries, computers, furniture, flights, tickets for concerts - all that at the click of a mouse. Opt for well-known companies or those with an address and phone number to avoid falling for any scams. Even your local independent stores might provide online services, please check with them. Many small-time shops too have WhatsApp shopping services now. You can buy from them as well at a time that suits you, rather than having to free up a Saturday morning.

Take A Break

Give yourself a holiday every week, or at least one day twice a week to recharge yourself. When you take a moment to put yourself first, you can spend time relaxing and unwinding, learning new things, being receptive and opening your mind to new possibilities, even practical things such as having your hair cut, choosing clothes that you love and feel good in. The choice is yours, but the point is... you have a choice.

The day you plan for yourself is to make you more special and alive by being in your own company.
• You're relaxed, calmer, happier and often more energetic.
• You're open to thinking about what needs to change when you get back home.
• You know what's worrying you the most so you know how to deal with it.
• You have breathing space to reflect on your life, the good bits and the not-so-good bits.
• You've opened your mind to new things.
• You've learnt about the world and the different people and places that make it tick.
• You've stepped away from your everyday life and taken a peek at what else is out there.

To make such a day, talk to your family and plan a day in 10 days for yourself. A day off need not necessarily mean for you to move out and about, make that day for yourself to do what you love to do. Not for anyone else, but for yourself. If you have the luxury, you can take a time off every day to make such a moment for yourself, which helps you relax. Realising that time for self-care is a priority and is non-negotiable is one of the best things that you could ever do to your inner self. By helping you to be in touch with your inner persona, you are helping your family too. Having a rejuvenated mind will help set the mood at home and bring out happiness your way. It doesn't have to be a complete day away, it could be an hour a day with a cup of coffee and your favourite book or a phone call with your favourite friend. Regardless of the way you spend it, making time for yourself is what matters.

Routines can make it easier and simpler to fit everything that you HAVE to do in it, so you have more time to do what you WANT to do. Plan your routines to make your life far more organised, moreover having planned routines will help your partner have the time to get what they can do for you. Find easy ways to plan and prepare the things you need to do such as housework, planning meals, even routines for your kids such as nap times and structured bedtimes.

Once in place, you'll know your daily schedule,

things will get done a little and often, if you miss a day it won't matter and you'll be able to make time for yourself again. Time for you whilst the baby naps, time for you when the kids are in bed, time for you instead of a backlog of housework, time for you whilst dinner is getting cooked as you've prepared and batch-cooked in advance.

Love yourself and do what you love to do every day. And get one day especially for you. If you love to move around alone or with your partner, plan it and make it happen. Life is sweet while you fulfil these little things that you love to do for yourself. Keep aside some time for your health and beauty, keep time for your friends and relatives. Keep time to watch movies, if you have it planned, you can find lots of time to make your life special for you. If you are working women, it will be a bit more challenging to make time for you but it's not impossible if you look to find a solution and plan smartly. When it comes to health and happiness, different people have different needs. But there are some universal truths. We all need the basics of sleep, physical movement, and sufficient food. And to thrive, most require quality time with people, time in nature, time for spiritual connection, and time doing something that brings joy.

Take a moment to define what you need and what you want. Ask yourself:

- Plan for your health. - What kind of physical exercise keeps you feeling in shape and healthy?
- Plan - How many hours of sleep is needed, to go to bed on time?
- What nourishment keeps up your energy and makes you feel full?
- Find the right people you enjoy spending time with.
- How can you find ways to make good time outside the home, and inside the home.
- How to drive out and have a great day with a friend?
- How can you connect with yourself and find your spiritual life?
- Activities that make you feel loved. - a hobby, reading, volunteering, or social help.

If you feel as though there is always more you could be doing, you'll need to consciously set aside time for self-care. As well you have to discuss with your partner the importance of getting a day for you in your life. No partner will say no to you if they understand that the time you are putting aside for yourself is even less than 1% time you put for your family. In doing so, you will clearly give yourself permission that this is the most important and appropriate thing to do now. Making time for yourself is making a way to keep yourself happy and motivated. That is important for the happiness of your family. Go for it and list out what you love to do and schedule it to get the goals to happen. You will enjoy your life the most while you are able to do things for yourself besides for your family.

About The Author

A M Kaywills

A. M KAYWILLS is the author of many motivational articles. Successful Married Life is his first published book in the English Language. Kaywills was born and raised in South India. He was a motivational activist before shifting his focus to motivational books. He's also penned fiction in his local language and is expected to get it published soon in English.

Your life and Marriage

In your life 70% of your life's growth is happening after the age of marriage, so it's very important that your partner has to be supportive to succeed each other in your life. The rule is if he is wealthy you have most advantages of financial freedom.

Most issues we face in married life are simple and common. But most of the couples don't have the experience to handle it positively.   Your success in wealth, health, and relationships all is very related to your married life success. If you can't fix your married life it's hard for you to fix your career life.

" This book is designed to make your life peaceful, lovely, and rich."

Printed in Great Britain
by Amazon

61698572R00047